I0478150

CONTENTS

DANIEL AYME

The Frequency of Prosperity: Tuning in to Financial Abundance

Daniel Ayme

INTRODUCTION

The Science and Philosophy of Prosperity

The idea that we can tap into the "vibration of money" may seem mystical or even a little abstract at first glance. However, behind this concept we find a rich combination of science and philosophy that can help anyone understand and, above all, apply the principle of abundance in their own life. *Getting into the money vibration is actually aligning with prosperity*, adjusting thoughts, emotions and actions so that they work in harmony, attracting the financial resources we desire. This involves both a theoretical understanding and a practical commitment - and it's this junction between science and practice that we're going to talk about.

The Concept of "Money Vibration"

But what does "money vibration" really mean? Think of the universe as an energy field where everything, including our thoughts and feelings, is in constant movement and vibration. When we talk about money vibration, we're referring to *a mental and emotional state that puts us in tune with the frequency of abundance and prosperity*. This approach suggests that, like a radio station, we need to adjust our own "frequency" to pick up financial opportunities and allow the flow of wealth to manifest in our lives.

This concept is not just philosophical; it is based on ideas that modern science is increasingly exploring, especially in fields such as quantum physics, neuroscience and positive psychology. Of course, *we don't attract money through positive thinking alone* - but the way we think and feel about money creates a magnetic field around us, influencing both our perception and our actions. So when we adjust our vibration to the frequency of prosperity, we are literally changing the way we relate to money.

The Link Between Thought, Emotion and Abundance

Many studies show that our emotional state directly affects the way we think and act, and this also applies to money. When we are in a state of fear or anxiety about finances, our brains operate at a survival level, which limits us to thinking about scarcity and making reactive financial decisions. On the other hand, *when we cultivate feelings of gratitude, security and confidence*, our brains activate areas related to creativity, problem-solving and balanced decision-making - all of which are essential for thriving financially.

Neuroscience has contributed to this understanding, showing that our thought patterns mould the connections in our brains. By repeating emotions and thoughts linked to abundance and gratitude, we create new neural circuits that help us realise financial opportunities where we previously saw obstacles. What's more, when we maintain a positive and prosperous outlook towards money, our brain releases neurotransmitters that make us feel good, which reinforces these patterns and creates a virtuous circle. In other words, *thinking about abundance isn't just an exercise in optimism; it's neural reprogramming that helps us align with the frequency of prosperity.*

Quantum Physics and the Reality of Abundance

Quantum physics has also brought interesting insights into the nature of reality and how our intentions can influence the world around us. In simple terms, quantum physics suggests that everything in the universe is made up of energy, vibrating at different frequencies. This means that our thoughts, feelings and even intentions are a form of energy that influences our environment. Although this concept may seem bold, it opens up the possibility that *our mental and emotional states actually shape the reality we experience*, including our relationship with money.

Of course, quantum physics is still a developing field and not everything is fully understood, but its principles have inspired innovative approaches to understanding how our mind interacts with the physical world. This science reinforces the idea that we are not just passive spectators of reality, but *active participants*, capable of influencing what happens to us. Applied to the concept of money vibration, this means that by intentionally cultivating feelings and thoughts of prosperity, we are, in a way, adjusting our financial reality.

Positive Psychology and the Science of Well-Being

Positive psychology is another area that has a lot to contribute to our understanding of prosperity. Developed to study what makes people feel fulfilled and happy, this science also investigates the role of positive thoughts, high emotions and intentions in our quality of life. Positive psychology studies show that people who nurture a vision of abundance in their lives generally achieve more financial success. This is no coincidence: *when we believe that we can achieve prosperity, our brains become more receptive to opportunities*, and our behaviour reflects this confidence.

Another interesting aspect of positive psychology is the practice of gratitude. Studies show that grateful people are more resilient and optimistic, and these characteristics are strongly linked to financial success. By practising gratitude for what we already have, we create a mindset of abundance that eliminates the fear of scarcity and allows us to make wiser financial decisions. *Gratitude helps us to focus on the positive in our lives, creating a stable emotional foundation for attracting more prosperity.*

Science and Philosophy Together

Combining these scientific studies with prosperity philosophies creates a powerful model for understanding how we can attune our vibration to that of money. It's not magic or wishful thinking; it's an approach based on knowledge of how our brain and emotional system work, combined with a philosophical view of the role of intention and energy alignment. From this understanding, each person can build their own prosperity strategy, putting these concepts into practice in their daily lives and noticing the changes they bring.

Getting into the money vibration is a process that requires practice and constant intention. But as we align ourselves with this state of prosperity, our financial life begins to reflect this new attunement. Science and philosophy together remind us that we are capable of moulding our financial destiny with our minds and emotions, creating a reality of true and sustainable abundance.

CHAPTER 1: UNRAVELLING THE WEALTH MENTALITY

"True wealth begins in the mind; money is only the consequence."

Our financial world is largely a reflection of the beliefs we hold about it. Often, the way we think about money can help us prosper or prevent us from achieving the financial success we desire. If you've ever wondered why some people seem to attract financial opportunities with ease while others struggle with scarcity, one of the answers may lie in the *limiting beliefs* you carry. This chapter is designed to help you identify and transform those invisible blocks that, without you realising it, are limiting the flow of prosperity in your life.

For many of us, talking about money is a delicate subject because it involves not only numbers, but also deep emotions, beliefs and even childhood memories. Limiting beliefs about money, even if we sometimes don't realise it, are formed from an early age and anchor themselves in our minds, shaping the way we see the wealth, opportunities and abundance around us. *So by transforming these beliefs, you are actually changing the way you relate to the financial world and the possibilities it offers.*

The Roots of Limiting Beliefs

First of all, let's understand what limiting beliefs are. A limiting belief is a thought or idea that you believe to be true and that restricts your potential for growth or fulfilment. In the case of money, these beliefs can take many forms, such as *"I'm no good with money"*, *"money is hard to come by"* or *"only lucky people get rich"*. They are like the sunglasses we wear to see the financial world - they distort reality, limit our vision and make us believe that we are incapable of prospering.

These beliefs usually stem from external influences: *it could be something we've heard from our parents, something we've seen in the media or difficult financial experiences we've had in the past.* For example, a person who grew up in an environment where money was constantly associated with financial worries and problems tends to develop a negative emotional relationship with wealth. Without realising it, they carry these impressions into adulthood, influencing every financial decision they make.

The Impact of Limiting Beliefs on Financial Flow

Imagine you're trying to fill a bucket with water, but the bucket is full of holes. No matter how hard you try, the water will keep leaking out and the bucket will never be full. So are limiting beliefs: they "leak" our energy and prevent us from prospering financially. *They block the flow of wealth, like invisible barriers we create to protect ourselves from fear, insecurity or change itself.* Sometimes this blockage occurs because we unconsciously fear financial success, thinking it will bring responsibilities we don't want or thinking we won't be loved if we are rich.

Studies show that the *scarcity mindset*, characterised by the belief that resources are limited and that there will never be enough, can directly influence financial behaviour. People with this mindset tend to avoid investments, stay in low-paid jobs or spend impulsively, fearing that the money will disappear at any moment. The good news is that these beliefs can be transformed.

Growth and Wealth Mentality: The Key to Prosperity

While limiting beliefs hold us back, the *growth mindset* propels us forward. This concept, widely studied in psychology, refers to the belief that skills, talents and even financial situations can be developed and improved with effort, learning and persistence. When we apply this mindset to money, we come to see wealth as something that can be built, regardless of circumstances. Instead of believing that we are born with financial luck or misfortune, we adopt the idea that we are *capable of shaping our financial reality.*

Science provides us with evidence that a growth mindset directly influences our success. People with this mindset tend to invest in financial education, seek out new opportunities and see financial challenges as learning opportunities. This translates into a greater ability to save, invest and multiply resources. And the most interesting thing: this kind of mentality can be learnt. Let's explore some exercises you can start doing now to develop your growth mindset and leave limiting beliefs behind.

Practical Exercise: Identifying Your Limiting Beliefs

Before you can transform your beliefs, you need to identify them. Take a quiet moment and do the following exercise:

1. **Write down all the phrases that come to mind when you think about money.** Don't filter anything; just write it down. Things like *"I don't have enough money"*, *"money is the root of all evil"*, *"rich people are selfish"*, and so on.

2. **Read each sentence and ask yourself: "Does this belief really reflect reality or is it just a thought I've been carrying**

around?" Often, you'll realise that these beliefs are the result of past experiences or other people's opinions, but that they have no real basis in the present.

3. **Transform each limiting belief into a positive and empowering affirmation.** For example, if you wrote "money is hard to come by", turn it into "money comes to me abundantly and naturally". Repeat these new affirmations daily to reprogramme your mind.

This simple exercise helps to *expose the roots of your financial beliefs and replace them with a new thought pattern.* Over time, you'll notice that your outlook on money will become more positive, which will open up space for new opportunities and achievements.

Cultivating a Growth Mindset: Step by Step

1. **Invest in Financial Education:** Learning about personal finance, investments and the economy is essential for developing confidence and making more informed decisions. With each new lesson, you reinforce the idea that you are capable of growing financially.

2. **Look at Mistakes as Opportunities to Learn**: If something has gone wrong, ask yourself: *what can I learn from it?* Every mistake can be a valuable lesson that brings you closer to your financial goals.

3. **Set Realistic and Attainable Financial Goals:** A growth mindset thrives on clear objectives. Set measurable goals and small milestones that you can fulfil, staying motivated and celebrating each achievement.

4. **Surround Yourself with People with a Growth Mindset:** Being around people who have a positive and prosperous outlook helps you adopt this mindset too. Join finance groups, read success stories and stay inspired.

Real-life example: Juliana's transformation

Juliana is a clear example of how changing beliefs can transform a financial life. From a young age, she believed that money was hard to come by and that in order to have a stable financial life, she would have to give up important things like time and freedom. When she started working, her spending was impulsive and the fear of never having enough made her make the wrong decisions. Juliana was trapped in a cycle of scarcity.

One day, reading about growth mindset, she decided to question these beliefs. She began to see money as a tool that could help her lead a better life, rather than something she should fear. *With this new vision, Juliana made an action plan, started studying finance, set clear goals and gradually changed her habits.* Today, not only has she achieved the financial security she was looking for, but she has also discovered that money can be a source of freedom and fulfilment, not fear.

Transform Your Beliefs and Transform Your Life

Unravelling the wealth mindset is a powerful process of self-discovery. With each limiting belief you overcome, you move closer to a financial reality that is more prosperous and in line with your desires. *Remember that you have the power to shape your relationship with money.* Like Juliana and so many other people who have dared to change, you too can open the door to prosperity by believing it's possible.

By applying these concepts and exercises to your life, you'll be taking concrete steps to transform your mindset and, as a consequence, your financial reality. After all, true wealth doesn't start in your bank account, but in your mind.

CHAPTER 2: ADVANCED FINANCIAL VISUALISATION

"Wealth begins in the mind, before it appears in any bank account."

Did you know that the way we imagine our financial life can literally mould our brain's connections to achieve success? This power of the mind to "create what doesn't yet exist" isn't just an artistic or intuitive skill; it's a process based on science and practice. Let's explore how visualisation can be the path to turning ideas into prosperous financial realities.

The Science of Financial Visualisation: Shaping the Brain for Success

Visualisation is a powerful exercise, and not just for those who practice high-performance sports or other concentration activities. When we repeatedly visualise the same scenario or goal, *our brain begins to treat this mental image as if it were a real experience.* Research into neuroplasticity, the brain's ability to reconfigure itself, shows that the brain doesn't distinguish well between what we vividly imagine and what we actually experience. It responds to both in the same way.

For example, a Harvard University study showed that people who repeatedly visualise a goal are more likely to achieve it. *This practice increases motivation and activates areas of the brain associated with planning and execution.* So, by using financial visualisation, you are actually "training" your brain to become more receptive to opportunities for prosperity and to perceive and seek out paths that lead to success.

The secret of financial visualisation is not to vaguely wish for money or just think "I want to be rich". Effective financial visualisation must be clear, detailed and emotional. It involves creating a scenario that connects the sensations of the mind and body, allowing you to mentally see yourself already achieving your financial goals and feeling the satisfaction and security that come with it. *"Be specific,"* many visualisation experts advise, because the more detail, the more realistic the mental image becomes, and the impact on the brain is intensified.

Guided Visualisation Practice: The Power of Mental Imagery with Intention

To make this technique work, you can use guided visualisation, a practice that leads the mind through a well-guided and focused process. Try dedicating a few minutes a day to a guided visualisation practice to strengthen your "mental muscles" of wealth. Let's do an exercise:

1. **Choose a quiet, comfortable place** where you can relax without interruptions.

2. **Close your eyes and breathe deeply** three times, focusing on each inhale and exhale.

3. **Imagine a specific scene** in which you have already achieved the financial freedom you desire. Think about the details: *where you are, what you're doing and who you're with.* Feel the joy and gratitude of living in that moment.

4. **Connect with body sensations**. Feel the calm, confidence and satisfaction in your body, as if that moment were real.

5. **Practise repeating this visualisation every day**. If possible, do it at the same time to create a mental routine.

This type of practice may seem simple, but its effects are profound. Studies show that repeating visualisations increases neuroplasticity and reinforces the neural connections that favour goal-oriented behaviour.

Creative Visualisation Techniques: Exploring New

Ways of Thinking about Wealth

In addition to guided visualisation, there are creative ways to extend the practice and integrate it into your daily life. Consider creative visualisation as a way to make the process even more impactful and enjoyable. Some approaches that can help include:

- **Financial Vision Boards**: Set up a vision board that is visually inspiring, bringing together images that represent your financial goal. It could be a picture of your dream house, car or workplace. Hang it up in a visible place so that you can look at it every day and remind yourself of your goal.

- **Visualisation Diary**: Keep a notebook or diary in which you describe your financial future in detail, as if it were already happening. *Use the present tense*, for example: "Today, I have an abundant and comfortable life. Each month, new resources come in and I continue to move forward with financial security."

- **Exploring the Senses**: When visualising, try to involve all your senses - think about how it feels to touch the steering wheel of your new car, to hear the sound of your house in a quiet neighbourhood, to smell the aroma of an inspiring work environment. This practice reinforces the mental images even more.

- **Visual Meditation for Wealth**: Practise a meditation focused on wealth, starting with breathing and moving on to a specific visualisation. Imagine money flowing healthily into your life, with each note and coin arriving with fluidity and constancy.

These practices help to solidify visualisation, creating an almost tactile experience of your goal. It is this clarity that drives the brain to work towards what it perceives as a tangible reality.

Case Studies: Visualisation in Real Life

Want to know how it works in practice? Let's take a look at some inspiring examples that show how visualisation has been a real tool for change for those seeking prosperity.

Sara, a budding entrepreneur, was struggling to establish her business. Everyone told her that the market was too competitive, but she felt there was a place for her idea. Determined, Sara started practising financial visualisation. Every day, *she saw herself signing contracts, receiving payments and watching her business flourish.* In less than a year, her visualisation practices, combined with hard work, turned into reality: her business was thriving and she was expanding her market.

Another example is that of *Rafael*, an employee who dreamed of improving his financial situation in order to provide stability for his family. He used a guided visualisation technique, focusing daily on seeing himself in a better financial position. Months later, Rafael reported new motivation in his work and an increase in his savings. He says that by visualising success, he began to see more opportunities and take calculated risks, such as investing in courses that qualified him for promotions.

These cases illustrate that visualisation is not just a mental exercise, but a practice that reinforces positive behaviour and assertive decision-making, bringing people closer to their financial goals.

Practice and Persistence: Implementing Visualisation in the Routine

Consistent practice is essential for visualisation to be truly effective. *The key is persistence.* Visualising your goal once or twice can help, but it's the continuity that makes the mental image establish itself in the subconscious, influencing daily choices.

Here's a step-by-step guide to how you can include financial visualisation in your routine:

1. **Start the Day with a Short Visualisation**: As soon as you wake up, take two minutes to visualise your ideal day. Imagine the financial opportunities arising and the actions you will take to capitalise on them.

2. **Night-time visualisation**: Before you go to sleep, take a few minutes to mentally review your long-term financial goal. Reinforce the visualisation of what you want to achieve.

3. **Reaffirmation During the Day**: Whenever

possible, mentally reaffirm your vision. Small reminders throughout the day strengthen your commitment to your goals.

4. **Weekly Complete Visualisation Practice**: Choose one day of the week to do a complete visualisation, where you can really dedicate yourself and visualise every aspect of your financial goal in detail.

Cultivating a Prosperity Mindset with the Money Frequency

Visualising is also a way of attuning your mindset to the frequency of money, a concept that suggests that thoughts of abundance attract prosperity. *Imagine the frequency of money as a wave of energy that responds to our thoughts and emotions.* When your mind and body tune into this energy of abundance, you tend to act in a way that is more open to new financial opportunities.

When you connect with the frequency of money, visualise yourself not just achieving a specific number or goal, but feeling secure, satisfied and deserving of everything that comes your way. This practice, over time, strengthens self-confidence and optimism, propelling you into inspired action.

Financial visualisation is much more than an exercise in imagination. It is a powerful tool that transforms the mind and brain to see, attract and create opportunities for wealth. By training your brain with clear, detailed visualisations, you not only reinforce your desire for prosperity, but also prepare yourself to embrace the chances that come your way.

CHAPTER 3:
THE ENERGY
OF GRATITUDE
AND MONEY

"Gratitude doesn't make your bank account richer, but it transforms the way you see and deal with money."

How many times have you been grateful for the money you have, for what you've already achieved, or even for what's still on the way? In everyday life, we often focus on the lack, the bills to pay and the fear of not having enough. But what if I told you that the secret to a more prosperous financial life actually lies in gratitude? Gratitude is more than a passing emotion; it's a practice, a way of attracting positive energy and changing the frequency in which you live, which consequently impacts your relationship with money.

Gratitude as a Catalyst for Abundance

Science and spirituality have something important

in common: both tell us that what we focus on tends to grow in our lives. *When we give thanks for what we already have, we are, in essence, signalling to the universe (or to our own mind) that we deserve and are ready to receive more.* Gratitude then becomes a magnet, a catalyst for abundance.

Imagine money as a plant that you cultivate. If you neglect it, complaining that it doesn't grow fast enough, the plant tends to wither. However, if you water it with care and gratitude, it thrives. The same logic applies to money. When you see money as a limited resource, scarce and difficult to maintain, your energy to attract more of it diminishes. But by being grateful for every coin, every opportunity and every resource that comes your way, *you activate an energy that attracts more abundance.*

This principle is also supported by scientific studies that show that *practising gratitude reduces stress and increases well-being*, which can have a direct impact on our ability to make more assertive and conscious financial decisions. In a study carried out by the University of California, led by Robert Emmons, it was found that people who practise gratitude on a regular basis report fewer feelings of envy and greater satisfaction with their own lives, factors that indirectly influence even the way they deal with money.

Daily Financial Gratitude Exercises

Now, you may be asking yourself: "How can I apply

this practice of gratitude to my daily financial life?" I'm going to guide you through some simple but powerful exercises so that you can begin to feel this transformation.

1. Financial Gratitude Diary

Every night before you go to sleep, write down three things related to money or material resources that you are grateful for. It could be anything: a bill you managed to pay, a gift you received, or even the possibility of having a roof over your head. *This exercise will help redirect your focus to what you already have,* reducing your fear of scarcity and increasing your sense of fulfilment.

2. Acknowledge Every Payment

Every time you make a payment - be it a utility bill, a loan instalment or a purchase at the market - *say thank you.* It may seem simple, but this act transforms the payment from an "expense" to an "exchange of energy". By saying thank you, you remind yourself that this money is serving a purpose and thus create a more harmonious relationship with your finances.

3. Visualising Abundance

This exercise involves imagining the financial life of your dreams and giving thanks as if it were already a reality. *Close your eyes, visualise yourself in a comfortable financial situation and give deep thanks for it.* When you practise this visualisation with gratitude, your mind begins to work in favour of your financial goals, making decisions that are more in line with this vision of abundance.

These small gratitude rituals, when practised daily, have the power to transform your mindset and, over time, create a more positive flow of money in your life.

Scientific Evidence of the Impact of Gratitude

Gratitude is not just a spiritual or motivational practice; it also has solid scientific foundations. Studies show that gratitude can reduce levels of cortisol, the stress hormone, while increasing the production of dopamine, the "pleasure hormone" [Emmons & McCullough, 2003] . When we are calmer and more satisfied, we tend to make more rational and considered decisions - including financial ones.

Another interesting study, published by the American Psychological Association, showed that people who frequently cultivate gratitude have a more optimistic perception of life and a greater capacity for resilience in times of financial crisis. *In other words, gratitude not only improves our relationship with money, but also strengthens us to deal with the inevitable financial challenges that come our way.*

The curious thing here is that, according to this same research, people who practice gratitude are more likely to engage in saving and investing behaviours. *Why? Because gratitude promotes a sense of security and contentment with the present, which reduces the need to spend impulsively in the search for immediate gratification.*

A Step-by-Step Guide to Implementing Financial Gratitude

1. Start **a Morning and Evening Ritual:** Begin and end the day by giving thanks for one specific thing related to your financial well-being.

2. **Have a Symbolic Object:** Choose an object that symbolises abundance for you, such as a coin or a stone, and carry it with you. *Whenever you feel anxious about money, hold it and give thanks for what you already have.*

3. **Review your Finances with Gratitude:** Review your expenses and earnings for the month with the aim of finding reasons to be grateful. This exercise can help create a more positive relationship with money and reduce financial stress.

4. **Use Thank You Phrases: Make it** a habit to say thank you mentally or out loud every time you receive any money. Say something like: *"I am grateful for the money I have received, and I receive it with joy and wisdom."*

5. **Practise Conscious Generosity:** Donate a small amount or help someone in need. *Generosity is an extension of gratitude and creates a flow of positive energy around*

you, as well as reinforcing the feeling of abundance.

Stories of Transformation with Financial Gratitude

I want to share with you the story of Ana, a friend who always viewed money with a mixture of fear and dissatisfaction. She worked tirelessly, but the money seemed to "disappear" before the end of the month. When Ana started practising gratitude, she felt sceptical at first. How could she be grateful for something that always seemed to be lacking?

But little by little, she began to see changes. *She became grateful for every small financial victory,* such as being able to pay a bill without delay or saving a small amount. Within a year, she reported that her financial anxiety had reduced dramatically and that she had accumulated more savings than in previous years. Gratitude didn't magically "bring in" money, but it transformed her relationship with it, which made it easier to create new financial opportunities and behaviours.

Money as Frequency: Connecting with Abundance

Finally, it's important to remember that money is also a form of energy, a frequency. When you vibrate in tune with abundance, *abandoning fear and cultivating gratitude*, you naturally align yourself with the frequency of money. It's like a radio station: to hear a specific song, you need to tune in to the right station. Gratitude is the button that adjusts the tuning to a station of abundance.

Try this practice and see how it changes not only your relationship with money, but also the way you feel about yourself and life. *You have the tools to transform your financial life and create the abundance you desire.* Just start today, with a simple act of gratitude.

CHAPTER 4: AFFIRMATIONS AND MENTAL PROGRAMMING FOR ABUNDANCE

"You are what you believe you are. And what you believe defines what you attract."

Have you ever noticed how certain thoughts seem to guide our actions and even shape our reality? Often, these beliefs go unnoticed, working like automatic programming, engraved in our subconscious. And what are these beliefs? Nothing more than ideas, repeated over and over until they become part of us. Now imagine that you can consciously choose these ideas, replacing the old, negative ones with ones that reinforce prosperity and abundance. That's the magic of affirmations and mental programming. In this chapter, you'll learn how to create powerful affirmations to transform your relationship with money and reprogramme your mind for prosperity.

How Affirmations Work and Their Influence on the Subconscious

Affirmations are positive phrases that we intentionally repeat to influence our thoughts and emotions. But they are not just empty words; *they are tools capable of reconfiguring the subconscious.* When we repeat an affirmation, we are literally "hammering" an idea into our mind, and over time it becomes part of our belief system.

Our subconscious is a kind of "data bank" where all the experiences and beliefs we have acquired throughout our lives are stored. It absorbs what we repeat often and acts on this information, influencing everything from our decisions to the way we see the world. *That's why changing what we repeat mentally can rewrite the foundations of our reality.*

According to a study published by the American Psychological Association, people who repeat positive affirmations show greater resilience and self-confidence, which leads them to make decisions that are more in line with their goals. Applying this practice to your financial life is like planting seeds of prosperity in your mind, gradually changing the way you deal with money.

Formulating Effective Financial Statements

Now that you know what affirmations are, how can

you create ones that really make a difference? I'm going to share a practical step-by-step guide so you can build affirmations that resonate deeply with your mind and bring results.

1. Use phrases in the present tense

It's important that affirmations are always in the present tense, as if what you want is already happening. *Saying "I am prosperous" is more powerful than "I will be prosperous"*, because the subconscious doesn't understand the future - it responds to the present.

2. Be Specific

Vague statements like "I want to have more money" have less impact. Instead, focus on something more concrete, such as "I attract new income opportunities every day" or "I manage the money I receive well, and it grows constantly."

3. Add Emotion

Emotion is the fuel of affirmations. When you put emotion into a sentence, it becomes much more powerful, because your subconscious picks up on that intensity. Imagine yourself saying "I am worthy of all the abundance the universe has to offer" with joy and gratitude. *The more positive feelings you put into it, the deeper the imprint it makes on your subconscious.*

4. Avoid Negatives

Avoid negative words in affirmations, as the

subconscious tends to ignore the negation and focus only on the rest of the sentence. For example, "I don't want to be in debt" can be interpreted as "I want debt" by the subconscious. *Formulate the affirmation in a positive way, such as "I have total control over my finances and I thrive on them."*

5. Choose Affirmations Aligned with Your Values

If the affirmation doesn't seem authentic or doesn't make sense to you, it won't have the same impact. Affirmations should reflect your deepest values and beliefs. *For example, if you value freedom, use affirmations that emphasise how money increases your freedom and autonomy.*

Examples of Affirmations for Financial Abundance

Here are some suggestions for affirmations that you can start repeating every day. Choose the ones that resonate most with you or adapt them to create even more personal versions.

1. *"I attract wealth and prosperity constantly and abundantly."*
2. *"I am worthy and deserve all the abundance the universe has to offer."*
3. *"I manage my money wisely, and it grows every day."*
4. *"I'm grateful for all the financial opportunities that come my way."*
5. *"Every day I become more aligned with the frequency of prosperity."*

Try repeating these phrases as soon as you wake up and before you go to sleep. The idea is that these affirmations become part of your routine, as a daily reminder that you are on the path to abundance.

Proven Mental Reprogramming Methods for Prosperity

In addition to affirmations, there are techniques that help reprogramme the mind to attract and accept prosperity. I'm going to share three effective methods so that you can complement affirmations and accelerate your progress even further.

1. Creative visualisation

Creative visualisation is a powerful technique for building a clear mental image of the reality you desire. *It works like a film you play in your mind*, where you see yourself experiencing all the blessings of financial abundance.

To apply this technique, find a quiet place, close your eyes and start imagining yourself living the financial life of your dreams. Try to include as much detail as possible: *what do you see around you, how do you feel, who is with you?* The more realistic and engaging the visualisation, the more impact it will have on your subconscious.

2. Emotional Anchoring

Emotional anchoring consists of associating a strong emotion with an affirmation or visualisation. This method is widely used in

Neurolinguistic Programming (NLP) and helps to further reinforce the message in the subconscious. *When you create an emotional anchor, the affirmation becomes more powerful.*

Try associating a feeling of joy, gratitude or fulfilment with one of your favourite affirmations. To do this, simply say the phrase and, at the same time, remember a moment of great joy or gratitude. Over time, your brain will associate the affirmation with that emotion, enhancing the effect.

3. Self-Hypnosis for Abundance

Self-hypnosis is a powerful tool for accessing the subconscious and installing positive beliefs. You can do this by listening to guided recordings or even creating a self-hypnosis script with the prosperity affirmations you want most. *This method works because, in a state of hypnosis, the mind is more receptive to new ideas.*

To get started, sit down in a comfortable place, relax, and listen to a recording that focuses on abundance and prosperity. You can also record yourself repeating your affirmations and listen to them while you relax. Repetition and a calm state of mind make it easier to absorb new ideas.

The Language of Millionaires

An interesting fact is that people with great financial success often have something in common: *they use positive and optimistic language when talking about money and opportunities.* Instead of saying "I can't" or "I don't have enough", they say things like "I'll find a way" or "I can make it happen." This kind of language reflects a mindset of abundance, which in turn attracts more opportunities.

Harvard researchers found that this optimistic linguistic pattern not only boosts self-confidence, but also reduces stress and increases resilience, key factors for financial success [Seligman, 2002] .

A Step-by-Step Guide to Applying Reprogramming Techniques

Here's a practical guide so you can implement everything you've learnt in this chapter:

1. **Choose 3 to 5 powerful affirmations that resonate with you** and repeat them every day, morning and night.

2. **Practice creative visualisation for at least 5 minutes a day,** imagining yourself in a life of financial abundance.

3. **Create an emotional anchor** associated with your favourite affirmation. Feel really happy and grateful when you repeat it.

4. **Try self-hypnosis** with a guided recording or record your own affirmations. Listen to them in a moment of relaxation for greater absorption.

5. **Avoid negative or limiting language about money**, and replace it with words of abundance and possibility.

Success Stories with Affirmations and Mental Reprogramming

To illustrate the power of these techniques, I'd like to share the story of Carlos, an entrepreneur who had always struggled to achieve his financial goals. Carlos was sceptical about the power of affirmations, but decided to give them a try. He started with simple affirmations, repeating every day that he was capable and deserving of prosperity. Little by little, he noticed that his self-confidence increased and that he began to make bolder and more assertive business decisions. After a few months, he reported a significant increase in his income and a complete change in his outlook on life.

Remember: you too can transform your financial life and live in abundance. These techniques are like training for the mind - the more you practise, the stronger your prosperity mindset becomes.

CHAPTER 5:
THE POWER OF
DETACHMENT

"True power lies not in holding on, but in knowing how to let go."

It's curious how contradictory the concept of detachment can seem when we talk about attracting financial prosperity. For many, the idea of "letting go" or "detaching" from money sounds like a risk no one wants to take. After all, how could we get something if we let go of the need to have it in the first place? However, letting go is one of the keys to getting money flowing in your life. *By letting go of anxiety and obsession with financial results, you allow the energy of money to move freely, finding ways to reach you.*

Many spiritual traditions and mindfulness practices talk about the importance of freeing yourself from the bonds of attachment. And while this may seem like an abstract concept, there is a practical and scientific reason behind it. *When we are attached to a specific outcome, we create tension, and this tension closes our mind to alternatives and opportunities.* Have you ever noticed how, when you're obsessed with something, the chances seem slim? And conversely, when we're more relaxed, new opportunities seem to come more easily?

We'll explore how you can apply the power of detachment to your financial life in a practical and accessible way. We'll also see stories of people who have managed to transform their finances by understanding and practising detachment with wisdom and balance.

Why Detachment Allows Money to Flow

Firstly, it's important to understand what it really means to let go of money. It's not about despising its value or "abandoning" your finances. On the contrary, letting go is the act of freeing yourself from the pressure, anxiety and fear that obsessing about money can generate. When you're constantly worried about scarcity or the need to accumulate, your mind becomes closed and stagnant. *The energy of money needs freedom to circulate*, just like the air we breathe or the water that flows in a river. If you put a dam in the current, you block the flow.

In practical terms, financial detachment involves developing confidence in yourself and your abilities to attract resources. When you're not desperately fixated on controlling the flow of money, you gain the clarity and peace of mind to see opportunities that can bring prosperity. *Money flows where there is openness and a willingness to receive it without fear.*

Many people realise that obsessing about money can even drive away opportunities. A simple example: imagine that you are so preoccupied with saving every cent that you fail to invest in something that would really make a difference to your career. This attachment to "saving" can mean losing sight of a greater chance for growth. Detachment, on the other hand, allows you to make choices with clarity and long-term vision, instead of being guided only by the fear of missing out.

Financial Detachment Practices: Exercises and Techniques

In order to detach in a balanced way, it's essential to practise some techniques that will help you feel more secure and calm about your relationship with money. Here are some simple and powerful practices for implementing financial detachment:

1. **Define your financial goals, but let go of excessive control over them**

Start by setting clear goals for your financial life - *savings for emergencies, a specific amount for investments or a project you'd like to realise.* Once these goals are set, focus on taking consistent action, but without obsessively clinging to the result. Keep an eye on your goals, but trust that by following your strategies, the path will be built up gradually.

2. **Practise financial gratitude**

Letting go can be made much easier by practising gratitude. Do a daily or weekly exercise: *write down five positive aspects related to the money you already have in your life.* These can range from small achievements, such as paying a bill on time, to receiving praise for your work. *This exercise helps shift the focus from scarcity to abundance*, fuelling confidence that what you need is within reach.

3. **Develop the habit of donating regularly**

Giving is a practical and powerful way of letting go. And we're not just talking about large sums. It could be a small amount for a cause you believe in, or even helping a friend. *When you allow yourself to donate, you are signalling to yourself that you trust in your ability to earn more.* Studies show that giving activates areas of the brain related to well-being and the feeling of abundance. By practising giving, you automatically reduce your fear of loss and cultivate a calmer mindset towards money.

4. **Let money circulate consciously**

Practise "letting go". *When you receive an unexpected sum of money, think of conscious ways to use it, without anxiety about saving every cent.* This could mean investing in something you enjoy, an experience that enhances your well-being or a course to improve your skills. When you see the money circulating and coming back to you, it's easier to trust the flow of money.

Case Studies: Detachment in Practice

To better understand the impact of financial detachment, let's take a look at some inspiring stories that illustrate how this practice can transform lives.

Luiza was a woman who, after years of financial instability, started obsessively saving every cent, refusing even to spend on basic necessities, which ended up affecting her health and well-being. When she learnt about the practice of detachment, she started to establish a small "experience fund" - an amount earmarked for spending that really made her happy. Little by little, she realised that her relationship with money became lighter and that, paradoxically, *the less she clung to absolute control, the more opportunities arose.* Today, Luiza manages her money with more balance and reports that her confidence in herself and the possibilities around her have increased significantly.

Another example is that of *Carlos*, a young entrepreneur who, when he started his own business, felt great pressure to make an immediate profit. He says he spent sleepless nights planning every detail and constantly worrying about the cash flow. It was then that a mentor suggested he adopt a more detached mentality towards the business. *"Focus on offering the best service, and the return will come naturally,"* the mentor advised. Over time, Carlos began to practise detachment. He realised that by concentrating on providing a quality service and letting go of the anxiety about immediate returns, clients began to value his work more and the business flourished. Today, Carlos always repeats to himself: *"Trusting the flow is the basis of my prosperity."*

Transforming Mentality: The Balance Between Detachment and Responsibility

Letting go of money doesn't mean neglecting your financial life. On the contrary, *it's a balance between responsibility and trust*, which allows for a healthier relationship with money. Establishing a solid financial routine, such as planning and controlling spending, is essential. However, once this is done, detachment helps prevent pressure and fear from dominating decisions.

This balance can be compared to holding a ball of sand. *The more you squeeze your hand, the more sand escapes through your fingers*. It's the same with money: the more you cling to absolute control, the more opportunities can be lost. By loosening your grip a little, making the ball of sand lighter in your hand, you keep it safe but free to flow.

Here are some steps to balance detachment with responsibility:

1. **Review your goals periodically**: Plan your finances, but set intervals to review your goals and needs. This helps you stay focused without being suffocated by daily control.

2. **Practise confidence in yourself and your abilities**: Work to develop skills that increase your financial security, but trust that your efforts will bring results in due course.

3. **Avoid the fear of spending with purpose**: If you identify an expense that can really help your personal development or well-being, allow yourself to invest. The emotional and psychological return is also a form of prosperity.

Cultivating the Money Frequency through Detachment

By letting go, you begin to operate at a higher level of abundance and prosperity. *The frequency of money, as some call it, responds to the mentality of openness and fluidity.* When you trust the flow of money and your own worth, money flows naturally. On the other hand, when there is fear and tension, the flow is blocked.

Imagine the money frequency as a dance: when you're light and synchronised with the rhythm, the steps flow and become natural. *Just like dancing, in the flow of money you have to find the rhythm and let the movement follow.* Cultivating detachment is like tuning in to this frequency, allowing money to flow without you having to force every step.

Practise Detachment and Increase Your Financial Freedom

At the end of this chapter, I invite you to try applying these financial detachment practices in your daily life. The power of detachment is not in giving up your dreams, but in trusting the process and freeing yourself from the constant pressure for absolute control. *With the right balance between responsibility and trust, you allow the energy of money to flow more naturally, making prosperity a constant presence in your life.*

Detachment is not a practice of loss, but of gain - gaining freedom, confidence and clarity. By letting go of fear and attachment, you gain a new relationship with money that will help you build the life of abundance you deserve.

CHAPTER 6: ACTIONS AND PRACTICES ALIGNED WITH ABUNDANCE

"Prosperity is a state of being, but it is built through daily actions."

If you want to achieve true financial abundance, you need to realise that thoughts and affirmations are only part of the process. For money to flow easily and consistently, it is essential that your day-to-day actions are in harmony with this intention of prosperity. In other words, as well as cultivating a mindset of abundance, you need to align your financial practices with this new vision.

The good news is that you can start now, regardless of where you are. In this chapter, we'll explore concrete practices for attracting prosperity through conscious financial management, planning and organisation. Most importantly, you'll see how small daily actions can create a prosperous and lasting mindset.

Practical Financial Management Strategies to Attract Prosperity

When we talk about prosperity, we often think of luck, unexpected opportunities or even sudden gains. But in reality, financial prosperity is something we build. It doesn't matter how much money you have today; what matters is how you handle it. *Financial management is an essential tool for creating and maintaining abundance.*

1. set clear goals

The first practical action to attract prosperity is to set clear financial goals. *It's harder to prosper without a specific destination.* Imagine you're sailing aimlessly; anywhere seems satisfactory, but the truth is that you hardly ever reach the place you really want.

So start by listing your financial goals. Think about short-, medium- and long-term objectives. Ask yourself: *What do I really want to achieve financially in the coming months and years?* These goals could include building up an emergency reserve, buying a property, creating a retirement fund or even going on a dream trip.

By setting specific goals, you create a clearer vision of what you want. This is fundamental for your daily actions to start moving towards these achievements. In addition, studies show that the simple act of setting goals increases the chances of realising them [Locke & Latham, 2002] .

2. Organise your finances

Financial organisation is one of the pillars of prosperity. Without it, it's easy to lose control of your money, spend more than you should and constantly feel in a cycle of lack. To start organising your finances, write down all your expenses and income. Do this in detail, recording both the big expenses and the small day-to-day expenses.

Keep in mind that every dollar you spend must be aligned with your goals and the life you want to build. A very useful tool for organising your finances is the envelope method or creating spending categories. This simple practice helps you visualise where your money is being used and make the necessary adjustments.

Also, consider using personal finance apps or spreadsheets to monitor your income and expenditure. They make it easier to keep track and give you a clear picture of your financial situation. *The more you monitor your money, the easier it becomes to see how it can be put to better use.*

3. Adopt the Habit of Saving Consistently

Lack of prosperity often comes from a lack of savings habits. But the secret here is to start small. *Abundance is a journey, and you don't have to expect to have large sums of money to start a savings habit.* Try setting aside a small amount every month, even if it's only a token amount at first.

Studies show that those who save regularly, even in small amounts, manage to accumulate a significant reserve over time [Thaler & Benartzi, 2004] . This simple act of saving creates a mindset of abundance and generates greater financial peace of mind.

4. Create an Emergency Reserve

An emergency reserve is essential for anyone who wants to live prosperously. It represents security that allows you to deal with unforeseen financial events without jeopardising other areas of your life. To begin with, set a target amount for your reserve, usually three to six months of your monthly expenses. Saving for this reserve is an act of self-love and responsibility, as it guarantees that you will have support in unexpected situations.

5. Study about investments

Investing is one of the most effective ways of multiplying your money. The idea here is not to become an expert overnight, but to start familiarising yourself with the basics of the investment world. There are various options, from conservative investments such as savings and direct treasuries to riskier options such as shares and cryptocurrencies. *The important thing is to take the first step, even if it's in something small and safe.*

Remember that investing is not a game of chance,

but a strategy for generating long-term prosperity. As you begin to understand how the market works and seek out more knowledge, it will become easier to find investments that are aligned with your objectives and profile.

Financial Planning, Organisation and Investment

Financial planning is the first step towards aligning your actions with a prosperous life. Financial planning is an exercise in visualisation, action and commitment. *It lets you know where you're going and makes you make more conscious decisions about the use of your money.*

1. Create a Conscious Spending Plan

A powerful practice is to create a spending plan in line with your values and goals. This is not a "budget" in the restrictive sense, but a way of directing your money towards what really matters to you. By adopting this type of planning, you avoid unnecessary expenses and create more space to invest in what really pays off.

To create this plan, list your main fixed expenses, such as rent, bills and food, and add an amount for leisure and other interests. This way, you avoid the feeling of deprivation, but ensure that every expense is aligned with your goals.

2. Invest in Your Financial Education

Being well-informed is one of the main secrets to prospering financially. It's not about knowing everything, but about having a solid foundation and continually seeking new knowledge. Read books on finance, take part in workshops and watch educational videos. *The more you learn, the more confident you become in making decisions that increase your prosperity.*

An interesting fact is that, according to studies, people with greater financial knowledge are more likely to accumulate wealth throughout their lives, as they are able to make more informed and strategic decisions about money [Lusardi & Mitchell, 2014] .

How Small Daily Actions Create a Prosperous Mindset

Ultimately, prosperity is not just about big changes, but also about small daily attitudes that reflect an abundant mindset. I'm going to share some simple examples that you can apply in your daily life to strengthen your connection to abundance.

1. Practise Financial Gratitude

Giving thanks for what you already have is one of the most powerful habits for cultivating abundance. Every night, write down three things you are grateful for in relation to your finances. It could be a purchase that brought you satisfaction, extra income, or even the opportunity to learn more about investments. *Gratitude activates the brain to focus on the positive and attract more of it into your life* [Emmons & McCullough, 2003] .

2. Focus on Solutions

When a financial challenge arises, avoid the impulse to focus on the problem. Instead, think about the solutions. This change of focus helps to reduce stress and stimulate creativity. *Prosperous people have the ability to see solutions and remain resilient, even in adverse situations.*

3. Reflect and Celebrate Small Achievements

Every step you take towards abundance is worthy of celebration. Appreciate every small achievement, such as saving a little more in a month or investing for the first time. *Celebrating these small victories reinforces the mindset of progress and continuous growth.*

4. Donate Generously

One of the greatest secrets of prosperity is generosity. When you give, even in small amounts, you are telling the universe that you trust the flow of abundance. You also feel more prosperous when you realise that you have enough to share.

An Inspiring Example: Sofia's Story

Sofia is a young woman who, from an early age, learnt the importance of financial education. Even with a modest income, she always saved part of what she earned. Over time, Sofia learnt about investments and began to invest her money. In just a few years, her discipline and patience paid off: she gained financial independence and was able to realise several dreams.

Sofia's example shows us that, with simple and consistent actions, anyone can achieve prosperity. It's not about how much you have today, but about how you look after what you have and how much you believe in your ability to transform your reality.

CHAPTER 7: STAYING ON THE FREQUENCY OF ABUNDANCE

"True prosperity is not something we achieve, but a frequency in which we choose to live."

Living in abundance isn't just about money or material goods; it's about maintaining a mindset and state of mind that remains steadfast, regardless of external circumstances. But how is this possible? How can we sustain a frequency of abundance even in the midst of the financial challenges that inevitably arise throughout life?

In this chapter, we'll explore techniques that help to maintain focus and frequency on prosperity, even when difficult situations arise. We'll talk about the importance of dealing with ups and downs without getting off track, about mindfulness and meditation practices that cultivate a prosperous mindset, and about how the environment and people around us influence our ability to attract and sustain abundance.

How to Deal with Financial Ups and Downs without Getting Out of the Mood

One of the truths of life is that, like the tides, our finances also fluctuate. There will be times of plenty and times of restriction. *The secret lies not in avoiding the swings, but in how we respond to them.* When faced with financial difficulties, our first instinct may be fear, anxiety or frustration. However, these feelings, although natural, have the power to pull us away from the frequency of abundance, making it even more difficult to get through the moment.

To help you stay aligned, here are some strategies for dealing with these periods without losing focus on prosperity:

1. Embrace Uncertainty with Confidence

When you realise that scarcity is only a temporary phase, it's easier to remain at peace. Remember that financial success is not a straight line and that ups and downs are part of the journey. *Choose to see each challenge as an opportunity to learn and grow.*

An interesting example comes from the investment market. Experienced investors know that in times of crisis there are opportunities for growth. They remain calm and look beyond the immediate situation. In the same way, you can see downturns as a chance to improve your relationship with money and abundance.

2. Revisit Your Achievements

When you face a financial challenge, take a few minutes to reflect on everything you've achieved so far. *Remembering your victories and progress renews your confidence and helps keep your mind on the frequency of abundance.* Psychology studies show that focusing on what we already have generates a state of contentment and attracts more positive experiences [Emmons & McCullough, 2003] .

A practical technique for this is to keep an "Abundance Diary", where you write down achievements, gratitude and moments of prosperity. In difficult times, revisiting these notes can be a powerful reminder that prosperity is an internal state, and that you have experienced this energy many times.

3. Stay in Action

In times of crisis, fear often paralyses us. But *what really helps to get out of a difficult situation is action, even in small steps.* This could mean reviewing your budget, finding new sources of income or seeking financial counselling. Whatever the action, it helps you regain a sense of control and re-align with the frequency of abundance.

An example of this is something that many people do in times of financial difficulty: "unstuffing". Getting rid of what is no longer useful or necessary can have a positive effect on various areas of life, including finances. By selling items you no longer use, you create a sense of space and renew the energy around you.

Mindfulness and Meditation Practices Focused on Abundance

Practising mindfulness and meditation can be a powerful tool for staying on the frequency of abundance. Mindfulness means being present in the moment, with acceptance and without judgement. Meditation, on the other hand, is a practice that helps quieten the mind, reducing stress and promoting a state of tranquillity.

Research shows that mindfulness practices can help reduce anxiety and increase life satisfaction, factors that contribute to a mindset of abundance [Brown & Ryan, 2003] .

1. gratitude meditation for abundance

A simple and effective practice is gratitude meditation. To do it, find a quiet, comfortable place. Close your eyes and breathe deeply, focusing your attention on each inhale and exhale. After a few minutes, start reflecting on everything you already have and value in your life. Imagine yourself immersed in feelings of gratitude.

This simple practice reprogrammes your mind to perceive and attract more abundance. It's a way of training your brain to value what already exists, creating a solid foundation for attracting more. Studies indicate that gratitude activates areas of the brain associated with pleasure and reward, strengthening the sense of well-being and promoting prosperity [Fox   et al., 2015] .

2. Visualising Abundance

Visualisation is a powerful technique that uses mental images to generate sensations and stimulate the mind to achieve goals. To practice visualising abundance, imagine yourself living a prosperous life, in detail. *Visualise what you want to achieve, what your routine would be like, and feel the satisfaction of having achieved these dreams.*

By visualising regularly, you train your mind to perceive opportunities and to align your actions with your goals. This exercise is an effective way to stay motivated and connected to the frequency of prosperity.

3. Breathing Exercise for Emotional Stability

When financial anxiety strikes, an effective practice is conscious breathing. Inhale deeply for four seconds, hold the air for four seconds and exhale slowly for another four. *This technique helps calm the nervous system and reduces stress, keeping your mind clearer and focused on abundance.*

Surround yourself with Positive Influences and Environments

The influence of the environment on our financial mindset is a powerful, but often underestimated, factor. What you consume on a daily basis, be it conversations, news or environments, directly affects your emotional state and, consequently, your ability to stay on the frequency of abundance.

1. choose your companions well

Jim Rohn's famous phrase, "You are the average of the five people you spend the most time with", applies perfectly here. Surrounding yourself with people who share a positive outlook on life and prosperity can be a great differentiator. *When you live with people who value growth and abundance, it's natural to adopt this mentality.*

2. Consume Inspiring Content

What you read, listen to and watch affects your mindset. Choose content that promotes abundance, teaches about financial education and inspires self-knowledge. *Reading stories of people who have achieved prosperity and listening to motivational talks are ways to feed your mind with ideas that bring you closer to the frequency of abundance.*

3. Create a Space that Respects and Attracts Prosperity

Organising and taking care of your physical space is an often neglected practice, but one that can have a significant impact on your frequency of prosperity. A clean, organised environment that reflects your goals and values creates a sense of well-being. *What's more, the act of looking after your physical space is a reflection of the way you look after your financial life and your goals.*

One example of this comes from the practices of feng shui, an ancient Chinese philosophy that teaches how to organise environments to attract prosperity and well-being. According to feng shui, small adjustments to physical space can have a positive impact on financial and emotional life.

A Real Example: Marcelo's Story

Marcelo worked in a technology company, but he always felt that, despite his efforts, something was preventing his financial life from prospering. After learning about the frequency of abundance, Marcelo decided to implement small changes in his life. He started meditating regularly, visualising the prosperous life he wanted, and decided to reorganise his space, eliminating objects he no longer used.

In addition, Marcelo became involved with people who shared his vision of growth. Gradually, he noticed positive changes, such as growth opportunities at work and greater clarity about how to manage his money. *Marcelo's journey shows us that, with small daily practices, we can align ourselves with the frequency of abundance and transform our reality.*

CONCLUSION: YOUR NEW LIFE IN TUNE WITH PROSPERITY

In this journey towards the frequency of prosperity, we explore how we can align our thoughts, emotions and actions to connect with true and lasting abundance. As we've already discussed, prosperity isn't just about accumulating material wealth, but about achieving a state of balance and confidence, a mindset of abundance that allows us to see and utilise the opportunities that life offers us.

Firstly, we saw that the road to financial prosperity begins with becoming aware of our thoughts and beliefs about money. We often carry limiting beliefs that we have acquired throughout our lives and which create an invisible barrier between us and what we want to achieve. Overcoming these beliefs is a process that requires self-knowledge and intention. By challenging thoughts of lack and replacing them with positive and encouraging affirmations, you are already reprogramming your mind for a life of success and fulfilment.

In addition, we learnt that modern science, especially quantum physics and neuroscience, supports the power of our thoughts and intentions. This means that when we tune our thoughts to the frequency of prosperity, we actually create space for new opportunities and positive circumstances to enter our lives. Scientific evidence shows that positive thoughts and feelings of trust and gratitude have the power to change our perceptions and make us more receptive to opportunities.

Gratitude, one of the central themes of this book, not only improves our emotional well-being, but also directly influences our relationship with money. The practice of gratitude helps us develop a mindset of abundance and realise what we already have, reducing anxiety and fear of scarcity. Through gratitude, we can transform the act of dealing with money into a harmonious exchange, where each transaction is seen as a way of strengthening our life and our purpose.

Another important concept is detachment. Sometimes we become so fixated on certain outcomes that we end up limiting our own capacity for expansion and growth. Detachment teaches us to trust in the flow of life, to believe that what is ours will come at the right time. Letting go doesn't mean giving up on your goals, but rather making room for opportunities to arrive naturally and unexpectedly. This practice is essential for anyone wishing to tune into the frequency of prosperity, as it allows our energy to flow without blockages, increasing our capacity for attraction.

For financial prosperity to be sustained, practical and consistent actions are essential. It's not enough to think positively or visualise an abundant life if our financial practices don't reflect this state. Organising finances, controlling spending and saving regularly are indispensable practices. Just as a plant needs water and constant care, prosperity requires us to consciously look after our resources and goals. Adopting a responsible and organised attitude towards finances is fundamental for abundance to be a continuous and growing state.

Another point we explore is the power of visualisation. The ability to clearly imagine where we want to go and how we want to live is a powerful tool. Visualisation allows us to anticipate success and create a mental image that guides our steps towards our dreams. By frequently visualising a prosperous reality, we strengthen our goals and maintain the motivation to achieve them. Visualisation is not just a mental practice; it's a way of training our brain to act in alignment with our goals.

True prosperity also involves generosity and the desire to share. When we practice generosity, whether through financial donations, donations of time or donations of knowledge, we are connecting with a flow of abundance that values and respects others. This cycle of giving and receiving reinforces our healthy relationship with money and increases our confidence that we will always have enough for ourselves and those we love. Generosity then becomes a natural expression of abundance and a reminder that prosperity is a shared path.

Finally, the constant practice of these actions and values leads us to maintain the frequency of prosperity in all areas of life. When we are in tune with this frequency, our focus stops being solely on money and we start to live with a sense of fulfilment, purpose and peace. This doesn't mean that we will never face difficulties, but rather that we will be prepared to overcome them with resilience and serenity. Prosperity, in this sense, is a daily choice that involves a commitment to positivity, the practice of gratitude and confidence in our own value and ability.

I invite you, the reader, to continue on this journey, applying the teachings and practices we've explored to your life. Prosperity begins internally, in the way we think and feel, and is reflected in the choices we make every day. By cultivating a mindset of abundance, trust and gratitude, you will be adjusting your frequency to attract the opportunities, connections and experiences you desire. The prosperity frequency is more than a practice; it's a philosophy of life that can transform the way you relate to the world and to yourself.

May this book be a guide to help you live with purpose, in harmony with the abundance around you. And that, by entering this frequency, you discover a prosperity that goes beyond money, finding a true balance that allows you to achieve your greatest dreams and live a full and fulfilled life.

RECOMMENDED BIBLIOGRAPHY

This list contains works and authors cited and complements the ideas of prosperity, visualisation, neuroscience and detachment practices:

1. Neuroscience and Positive Psychology

- **"Positivity: Top-Notch Research Reveals the Upward Spiral That Will Change Your Life"** - Barbara Fredrickson
  Explores the impact of positive emotions on neuroplasticity, a concept central to reprogramming the mind for prosperity.

- **"The Power of Neuroplasticity"** - Shad Helmstetter
  This book covers how the repetition of thoughts influences mental reconfiguration, a cornerstone of Ayme 's book on prosperity.

2. Quantum Physics and Intention

- **"The Field: The Quest for the Secret Force of the Universe"** - Lynne McTaggart
  Discusses the quantum field and how our intentions influence reality, based on

principles explored in the book.

- **"The Quantum and the Lotus"** - Matthieu Ricard
and Trinh Thuan
Combines quantum physics and spirituality, expanding on the idea that we are co-creators of financial reality.

3. Law of Attraction and Visualisation

- **"The Power of Your Subconscious Mind"** - Joseph Murphy
This classic provides practical tools for financial visualisation and creating positive beliefs about money.

- **"Ask and It Is Given: Learning to Manifest Your Desires"** - Esther and Jerry Hicks
Expands on the concept of vibration and alignment with abundance, with practices for maintaining the frequency of prosperity.

4. Gratitude and Mindfulness

- **"Thanks!: How the New Science of Gratitude Can Make You Happier"** - Robert Emmons
Underlies the importance of gratitude and how it positively impacts financial and emotional life.

- **"Wherever You Go, There You Are"** - Jon Kabat-Zinn
Focuses on the practice of mindfulness to create a balanced and positive relationship with money.

5. Detachment and Prosperity

- **"The Art of Happiness"** - Dalai Lama and Howard Cutler
  Explores the philosophy of detachment and its relationship with happiness and well-being, concepts that support the flow of abundance.

- **"Letting Go: The Pathway of Surrender"** - David R. Hawkins
  Offers insights into emotional and financial detachment, demonstrating how letting go is an essential practice for prosperity.

6. Financial Planning and Financial Education

- **"Your Money or Your Life"** - Vicki Robin and Joe Dominguez
  Presents tools to transform the relationship with money and build a life aligned with personal values.

- **"The Richest Man in Babylon"** - George S. Clason
  This classic book provides practical and timeless lessons in financial planning and prosperity.

These books complement the teachings *of The Prosperity Frequency*, allowing the reader to deepen their knowledge of science, psychology, philosophy and spiritual practices to create a financially abundant and balanced life.